BLAVATSKY AND THE SECRET DOCTRINE

By MAX HEINDEL

Reprinted by Murine Press, 2008

Table of Contents

Table of Contents 2
INTRODUCTION i
CHAPTER I...x
CHAPTER II..12
CHAPTER III 15
CHAPTER IV 28
CHAPTER V..42
APHORISMS...52
Appendix A 56
Appendix B 60

INTRODUCTION

It would have been a real loss to all students of mysticism and metaphysics if this little essay on H.P. Blavatsky and "The Secret Doctrine" had not found its way into print.

Max Heindel, the Christian mystic, pays homage to Madame Blavatsky, the Oriental occultist. He sees above the little differences which divide the West from the East and rejoices in the great wisdom which has flowed forth out of Asia, rendering fertile the plains of the world's thought.

Great is the mind which rejoices in the greatness of other minds. Max Heindel's tribute to the memory and work of Blavatsky and her Masters is a truly beautiful gesture in a world little given, alas, to such gentle impulses.

We live a code of criticism and condemnation with small appreciation of the works of others. Sects and creeds build up walls about themselves, and only heroic souls in whom spiritual perceptions are truly awake can rise above these imaginary limitations. Think back over the books that you have read and recall how seldom it is that any writer speaks well of another.

Each man, firm in his own opinions, gives scant courtesy to the opinions of others. There are many teachers in this world who instruct with words, but only a few who instruct with the noble example of generous deeds.

In his textbook of Christian metaphysics, "The Rosicrucian Cosmo- Conception", Max Heindel refers to Madame Blavatsky as "a faithful pupil of Eastern Masters" and in the same paragraph he speaks of her great

BLAVATSKY AND THE SECRET DOCTRINE

book "The Secret Doctrine" as an "unexcelled work." With his deep appreciation of spiritual values Max Heindel was eminently qualified to recognize the fundamental merit of Madame Blavatsky's work. The Christian mystic is here revealed as a sincere student of Oriental occultism.

His summary of The Secret Doctrine in the latter part of this book reveals a remarkable grasp of the outstanding principles of the monumental spiritual traditions of Asia.

In a few brief and simple words Mr. Heindel sums up Cosmogenesis, the creation of the world, and Anthropogenesis, the creation of man. Both Rosicrucians and Theosophists, in fact all sincere students of the occult sciences, will benefit from a consideration of this summary.

The manuscript of this present book may properly be considered as Max Heindel's first literary effort. It was the beginning of a considerable metaphysical literature devoted to the application of mystical idealism to the living problems of s sorely afflicted mankind. It has been written that "the first shall be last."

This little book brings into print the only remaining unpublished manuscript of Max Heindel. The manuscript originally consisted of the notes of two lectures delivered before the Theosophcial Society in Los Angeles.

In the years which followed the preparation of these lectures Max Heindel greatly increased his store of mystical knowledge and has justly earned recognition as America's foremost Christian mystic.

Introduction

His reverence and respect for Madame Blavatsky in no way altered, however, and to the day of his death he always referred to her in terms of highest admiration. It was through the writings of Blavatsky that Max Heindel received in this life his first knowledge of occult sciences.

He recognized gratitude to be the first law of occultism and his fine soul preserved to the end a beautiful spirit of gratitude for the inspiration and instruction he had gained from the Secret Doctrine.

Both Madame Blavatsky and Mr. Heindel dedicated their lives to the service of mankind. Each was devoted to the dissemination of spiritual knowledge. Both were rewarded for the most part by ingratitude, persecution and misunder- standing.

Both suffered from the falseness of friends and learned how cruel the world can be to those who seek to educate and improve it.

Only the leader of a spiritual movement can realize how heavy a responsibility leadership can become. Madame Blavatsky had already passed into the invisible world before Max Heindel began his ministry. They never met upon the physical plane.

Though denied personal acquaintance with the great Oriental occultist, Max Heindel came to understand Blavatsky through years of similar service to the same high ideals. He came to understand her as only a mystic can, and his appreciation of her loyalty and her patience was deepened by the adversities which he himself endured.

Both H.P Blavatsky and Max Heindel gave their lives in a beautiful service to the spiritual needs of the race.

BLAVATSKY AND THE SECRET DOCTRINE

Both went to early graves, broken by responsibility and persecution. Each has left as a legacy to unborn generations a metaphysical literature which shall survive the visissitudes of time.

The true purposes of mysticism are to perpetuate, interpret and apply the idealism of the race. Men turn to religion for guidance, encouragement and solace. We want religion to stand back of us when we try to live honest lives.

We want to know that there exists somewhere in the world a body of united people who are upholding spiritual values in a world of crumbling material manifestations. We are all seeking inspiration.

We want ideals. We want a worthy purpose to unite us in action. We desire to establish in this vale of tears a spiritual structure which shall be elevated above the humdrum. We want to go out into life recognizing our spiritual institutions as oases in a desert of materialism.

Civilization is in the throes of a great reconstruction period. As never before in recorded history men are seeking solutions to imminent and eminent problems. Church and State alike are reaching out to grasp something that is ecure, something they may cling to when the world they have known passes into oblivion.

In all parts of the civilized world there are men and women devoted to mystical interpretations of life. These men and women are dedicated to a code of spiritual ethics which has as its foundation two great principles: the Fatherhood of God and the Brotherhood of Man.

Introduction

These students are for the most part organized into various groups large and small for the express purpose of self-improvement and social betterment. Such groups may be classified under two headings: First, those whose inspiration is fundamentally Christian; and second, those essentially Oriental.

While these groups are divided, by emphasis, the fundamental purposes which they seek to attain are identical, for all enlightened religious movements have as their chief aim and purpose the regeneration of man, individual and collective.

Max Heindel was a pioneer in Christian mysticism and Madame Blavatsky was a pioneer in Oriental occultism. Both established systems of thinking which spread rapidly throughout a soul-hungry humanity.

Not only did they leave organizations of their own, but the seeds which they planted in the hearts of men have sprouted forth and borne fruit in many parts of the world, where other organizations have been established along similar lines.

There is a considerable body therefore of mystics and occultists in America and their number is increased each day by earnest men and women whose hearts and minds are crying out for some reasonable explanation for the changes which are occurring in society.

Nearly all students of the occult sciences in America know the work which Madame Blavatsky and Max Heindel have accomplished. The lives of these two religious founders are a constant challenge to greater spiritual effort and more unselfish devotion. If we admire these great leaders we shall desire to further their work by the intelligent perpetuation of their doctrines through word and action.

BLAVATSKY AND THE SECRET DOCTRINE

During the period of the great Wrold War metaphysics lost a great opportunity to make a permanent contribution to the race by allowing itself to be broken up by internal disruptions and controversies. Organizations which should have been dedicated to the unselfish service of mankind instead wasted their energy in vain wranglings over personal issues of little if any importance.

Our present crisis is far greater than the World War. The whole civilized world is struggling against selfishness and corruption. A new and great opportunity is at hand for the application of spiritual solutions to material problems.

It is the duty of all spiritually enlightened individuals to forget all differences, sacrifice all personal ambitions, and rededicate themselves to the great ideals which brought their various orders and societies into existence.

During the great boom period immediately preceding the present economic crisis even mystical organizations were infected by the bacilli of wealth, personal ambition and exploitation. Personalities eclipsed principles and individuals and organizations departed from those simple truths which are the essentials of intelligent living.

Then came the collapse. Material values dropped like plummets to an unfathomable depth. Ambitions were scattered to the winds and the race was confronted with problems which can only be solved through a restatement of spiritual values and a rededication of men and organizations to principles of enlightenment and truth.

Introduction

Suppose this very day H.P. Blavatsky, the lioness of the Theosophical Society, should return from the Amenti of the wise, and should demand an accounting from the members of the society she had founded.

Who could stand before her and say honestly, "Beloved teacher, we have done our best, we have remained true to you and the Masters for whom you spoke." How many could say, "We have been honest, kind, just and impersonal; we have hewed true to the wisdom you gave us; we have spread your message; we have read your books; most of all we have remained absolutely free, as you bade us, from all disastrous entanglements and alliances."

How many could say, "Here is your Society as clean as when you gave it to us." Could Theosophists do this or would they become abashed and unable to gaze into the great sad, luminous eyes of the first and Greatest Theosophist?

Could Madame Blavatsky walk through the corridors of Adyar and turn to those who represent her in the twentieth century and say, "Well done, good and faithful servants?"

If she could not say this, why not? Is it because they have remembered her name and forgotten her work? Is it because weak, petty men and women have so forgotten the greater good that they have elevated themselves to power upon the wreakage of ideals?

Theosophists of the world, rededicate yourselves to the noblest spirit that was among you, whose labors are your wealth, whose ideals are your purpose, and whose unselfish sacrifice is the cornerstone of your organization.

BLAVATSKY AND THE SECRET DOCTRINE

Suppose, in the same spirit, that Max Heindel returned to the fields of his earthly labors and in simple gabardine walked among his followers. Suppose he should say to them, "Brothers and sisters, have you loved one another? I planted a rose garden of virtues; have you tended it carefully?

My name is upon your lips, but is my work in your hearts? Have you been true one to the other? Have you labored unselfishly, impersonally? Have you so greatly loved our Heavenly Father that you have loved all men also?"

How would The Rosicrucians answer him? Could they say, "Beloved Brother, our constant inspiration, we have fulfilled your works in humility and gentleness.

There has been no pride among us, no selfishness, no personality, no small ambitions at a great cost. Here is the Fellowship you gave into our keeping. We can return it as beautiful, as clean, as united in holy purpose as you intended it to be.

There is no jot and tittle observance here; we are united not in petty things but in great things. In the fifteen years since you passed away into greater life we have sought to do your work.

We are as you intended us to be-- men and women in whom there is no guile." Would these words be true? If not, why would they not be true? Is man too weak to carry on a good work? Is his littleness so great and his greatness so little?

If we should feel ashamed if our leaders should return to us again and we should know that we have failed

Introduction

them, let us rededicate ourselves to them. Let the spirit of H.P. Blavatsky be reborn in the heart of each Theosophist and the spirit of Max Heindel live again in the heart of each Rosicrucian.

When this time comes, and may it come, the mystics and the occultists of the world can clasp hands across the gulf of their differences and, united in purpose, be an army of spiritual reconstruction marching like the prophets of old in the vanguard of progress.

-Manly P. Hall

1933

CHAPTER I

THE SECRET DOCTRINE is one of the most remarkable books in the world. I realize how far beyond my feeble powers is the task of conveying an adequate idea of the teachings contained within its covers. It has a history, however, a history of peculiar interest to the student who from its rich store seeks to garner the wisdom which, as the apostle has said, is like meat fit only for the strong.

How it came to be written, and under what circumstances it was written, and under what circumstances it was written, is the topic of this book. I shall endeavor to give in as simple and comprehensive language as possible an outline of the plan upon which the work was built and the teaching it reveals.

The nature of the task is such that I am forced to quote freely from Theosophical literature, especially from Colonel Olcott's *"Old Diary Leaves"*, Countess Wachmeister's *"Reminiscences"*, *"The Secret Doctrine"* itself, and other works.

It is first necessary for us to realize that Madame Blavatsky, or as she liked to be called, H.P.B., was, as she herself often expressed it, only the compiler of the work. Behind her stood the real teachers, the guardians of the Secret Wisdom of the ages, who taught her all the occult lore which she transmitted in her writings. She had a threefold ability which eminently qualified her for the task.

Introduction

First, she was able to assimilate the transcendental knowledge which came to her. Second, she was a worthy messenger of the Masters. Third, she had a marvelous aptitude for rendering abstruse Eastern metaphysical thought into a form intelligible to Western minds, and for verifying and comparing Eastern Wisdom with Western Science.

She also deserves great credit for her high moral courage in representing to the world thoughts and theories wholly at variance with materialistic science. Many of these teachings, however, have since been verified by science.

CHAPTER II

Humankind has always persecuted, tortured, and killed those who in thought have been in advance of their age. Witness Copernicus, whom only a natural death saved from a fate similar to that which half a century later overtook Bruno. Galileo was harassed all his life, and finally when old and broken in body and spirit by the abuse of the clergy, was forced to retract on his knees all of his teachings which was at variance with the commonly accepted views of the time.

The same fate was shared by countless others. The seed which these men had son, however, was not only indestructible, but grew and grew until one day the world woke up to find that what once was denounced as heresy had become the commonly expressed opinion.

Then came the epilog of the drama--when a Thorwaldsen immortalised in marble the same Nikolas Copernicus who, once persecuted, was proudly claimed as her son by Russia, or when amid the cheers of his countrymen was reared the statue of Giordano Bruno on the same spot where fanatical monks had danced around his funeral pyre and burned the genius in the name of God.

 At one time in the history of the West, men were scourged for the sake of the Christian religion. When Christianity became strong, it attempted to suppress science, which was then but a fledgling. Science, however, grew stronger and stronger, gradually forcing the Church into its present apologetic attitude.

Then the world slowly sank into a state of unbelief. Nothing which could not be weighed or measured was accepted. Anyone who dared to assert the existence of anything superphysical was at once stamped as an impostor. Science and religion vied with each other in their efforts to heap obloquy and opprobrium on such individuals.

With the foregoing in mind, we can better appreciate the great moral courage of H.P.B., and see why that courage constituted one of her qualifications as a messenger of the Masters.

In the same materialistic attitude of the world of that day is also to be found the reason for making use of phenomena. Many thoughtful persons have sincerely regretted that this part of the subject should ever have been taken up by the Society, but H.P.B. always maintained that in the early days of her work these proceedings were absolutely necessary.

This opinion was changed in the last years when the Master himself told her that phenomena had been a hindrance rather than a help to "The Secret Doctrine" in Europe and that it would have been better had only the philosophy been given.

In 1884 it was thought among the leaders of the Theosophical Society that the time had arrived for a revision and an amplification of Madame Blavatsky's first book *"Isis Unveiled"*, and that she was to rewrite it, with the late T. Subba Row as co-editor. All through the year they collected material. Then Colonel Olcott and Mr. Cooper-Oakley formulated a plan, and it was announced that the work would be published in twenty parts of about seventy-seven pages each. But on the 8th of January, 1885, H.P.B.'s Master communicated to her the scheme of *"The Secret Doctrine"*, and as a result, the original plans were abandoned.

Soon afterwards the heart trouble from which Madame Blavatsky was suffering became so serious that her physician, Dr. Mary Scharlich, insisted upon her leaving India if she would save her life. Acting upon this advice, H.P.B. left Adyar, the spot she loved most on earth, in the spring of 1885.

We next find her installed in a cheap little inn on the northern slope of Vesuvius. The room is almost bare of furniture, the floor is of stone. Through the crevices in windows and door blows a cold wind which aggravates the rheumatism of the poor "old lady" as she sits writing at her rickety old table far from friends, alone in a foreign country, the language of whose inhabitants she did not understand, sick in body, and chafing under the injustice done her by those whom she had befriended. Thus, inauspicious were the circumstances attending the first work on *"The Secret Doctrine"*.

In the fall of 1885 she went to the quaint old German town of Wurzburg. What associations this name calls forth--thoughts of Martin Luther, the stern and unflinching reformer who vowed against the Romish priests though the roofs of the city were covered with devils.

Not more staunch and unflicnhing was he than this new reformer who with dogged persistence, despite sickness and adverse criticism, toiled at her desk from day to day when she might have had ease and comfort.

CHAPTER III

Some time after Madame Blavatsky arrived at Wurzburg she was joined by the Countess Wachmeister, who loyally and lovingly helped in the great work. The number of visitors caused H.P.B. in a letter to a friend to write that the city was becoming a philosophical Medina. Continuing, she wrote:

"I am only in the middle of Part One, but shall in a month send you the first six sections. I take from **ISIS** *only facts, leaving out everything in the shape of dissertations, attacks on Christianity and Science--in short, all the useless stuff, and all that has lost its interest. Only myths, symbols and dogmas, explained from the esoteric point of view. It is actually and de facto a new work entirely. Cycles are explained from the occult side."*

Her insight into problems of philosophy, racial origins, fundamental bases of religions, and keys to old symbols was phemonenal; yet it was not the result of study, for never was a student more eccentric and restless. Of trained literary faculty she had none. She wrote under inspiration; thoughts flashed through her brain like meteors.

Scenes often painted themselves before her mental vision and died out when only half caught. Because of her excessive use of parentheses, many sentences were inordinately long. Like Shakespeare and other geniuses, she would take material where she found it, and work it into the mosaic upon which she put the stamp of her own individuality, and around which she wove the golden web of her own high powers.

In one of her letters she announced that the enormous volume of introductory stanzas, the first chapter on the Archaic Period and Cosmogony, was ready. *"But now,"* she goes on, *"how send them to Adyar? Suppose they are lost! I do not remember one word of them and so we would be cooked!*

Well---has read them through twice and started the third time. He has not found one part to be corrected in the English, and he says he is amazed at the gigantic erudition and the soundness of it, showing the esotericism of the Bible and its incessant parallels with the Vedas and Brahmanas. This is a little more wonderful yet than ISIS, that you corrected and Wilder suggested. Now I am absolutely alone with my armchair and inkstand and no books to speak of. In about four hours I wrote a whole section and the introduction of a whole Stanza (about forty pages) without any books around me. SIMPLY LISTENING-- simply listening."

Can we realize what that means? *She was merely writing* what was transmitted to her clairaudiently, as Colonel Olcott and others had seen her do day to day. Herein lies the answer to the traducers who have accused her of plagiarism. I am satisfied that never in one instance was she guilty of having consciosuly appropriated another's writings.

She may, however, have drawn them direct spiritually, or having received them second-hand from that great store- house of human thought and mental products, the Akash, where, as drops are merged in the ocean, personal begetters of thought are lost in the infinite Mind, save to those most advanced intelligences who can count the sand grains or the drops in the ocean and pick out the atoms in their vortices.

About December, 1886, Colonel Olcott received the first volume of *"The Secret Doctrine"* for revision by T. Subba Row and himself, but Mr. Row refused to do more than read it, saying that if he touched it he would have to rewrite it, as it was full of mistakes. This was mere pique, but it had its effect, for when his remark was reported to H.P.B., she was greatly distressed. She set to work revising the manuscript carefully, correcting many errors due to slipshod literary methods, and with the help of friends, especially Bertram and Archibald Keightley, put the book into the shape in which it was first published.

She was always eager to have her mistakes pointed out, and was also ready to correct them. The errors occurred especially in such of her writings as were not dictated to her psychically by the Master.

Frequently she would ruthlessly destroy faulty pages. Often at a word from the Master she would consign to the flames reams of laboriously prepared and copied manuscript, to the intense grief of her friends. Countess Wachmeister related that one day when she went into Madame Blavatsky's writing room she found the floor strewn with discarded manuscript.

To her question about it, H.P.B. replied, *"Yes, I have tried twelve times to write this one page correctly and each time Master says it is wrong! I think I shall go mad writing it so often, but leave me alone; I will not pause until I have conquered it even if I have to go on all night."* The Countess brought her a cup of coffee to refresh her and then left her to pursue her weary task.

An hour later Madame Blavatsky called her and said the task had been accomplished. The labor had been prodigious and the result small, as was often the case when she had been annoyed.

This is apparent from her answer to the Countess' question as to how she could make mistakes in setting down what was given her. She replied, *"Well, you see, it is like this. I make what I can only describe as a sort of vacuum in the air before me and fix my sight and my will intently upon it, and soon scene after scene passes before me like the successive pictures of a diorama; or, if I need a reference, as information from some book, I fix my mind intently, and the astral counterpart of the book appears and from it I take what I need. The more perfectly my mind is freed from distraction, the more easily I can do this, but after the annoying letter I had this morning I could not concentrate properly, and each time I tried I got the quotation all wrong. It is all right now, however, so Master says."*

H.P.B. often asked her friends in various parts of the world to verify quotations from books which could be found in libraries where such friends resided. Thus, she would need verification of a passage from a book of which only one copy was extant and that in the Library of the Vatican. Again, a friend in London would be asked to verify a quotation from some document possessed only by the Britich Museum. It should be noted, however, that she needed only VERIFICATION. The subject matter she already had.

Madame Blavatsky stated that she was only the mouthpiece of the Masters-- writing, speaking, and acting, as directed by them. This has been ridiculed and she herself caracterized as a rogue and an impostor. There are, however, certain incontrovertible facts to be taken into consideration by those who wish to form a fair and unbiased opinion.

When she wrote "The Secret Doctrine" she had around her only a handful of ordinary books. From such sources she could have obtained but little to help her. We cannot in this way account for the extraordinary and prodigious knowledge manifest in *"The Secret Doctrine"*.

Most of the time during which the work was written, she was hundreds of miles from any library of consequence. Had she been able financially to travel from library to library she would have been physically unable to seek out the passages she is accused of having plagiarised. She never said that she discovered the knowledge she gave the world. Her contention was that it came from the remote past; that it is in every scripture and in every philosophy.

The purpose of *"The Secret Doctrine"* is to quote from every scripture of every religion, from the writings of every people, in order to show the identity of the teachings and prove the antiquity of the subject-matter. What is new in the book lies not in the NATURE of its facts or ideas, for these can be found scattered among the works of various Orientalists and in the numerous sacred books which have long existed.

What is new is the selection by H.P.B. from all sources of facts which together form a single mighty concept of the evolution of the universe and of man--the coherent synthesis of the whole cosmogony. She qualifies as the greatest Teacher of the time because she had real knowledge and not mere book learning. She had that which enabled her to gather from many books in many places the truths which, fitted together, made one great whole. She held the clue which she was able to follow with unerring accuracy through the maze, and show that each individual material held within itself the possibility of becoming the single edifice.

Her work is the more extraordinary because she did it without being a scholar; without having had the education whcih would have fitted her to some extent for piecing together this knowledge; because she did what none of the Orientalists have done with all their learning, what not all of them together have done with all their knowledge of Eastern tongues and their study of Eastern literature.

Not one of them out of such a motley of material was able to synthesize such a momentous work. Not on of them out of that chaos was able to build up a cosmos-- but this Russian woman with little education did it. She who was no scholar and did not pretend to be one, somewhere gained a knowledge that enabled her to do what no one else--scholar or sciolist--has done. Somewhere she received that which made it possible for her to transform chaos to order and to produce a work which conveys to us an understanding of the universe and man.

She said it was not hers. She frequently spoke of her own lack of knowledge, and referred to THOSE who taught her. This brings us to the other part of the attacks made on Madame Blavatsky, or rather on the Masters, the existence of whom is regarded as a myth.

The learning and ability which she herself disclaims is not challenged by her enemies. They sometimes say that her knowledge is poorly digested, that she arranges her material badly, that her writings are misty, involved, self- contradictory. But that she possessed an extraordinary fund of varied knowledge bearing on out-of-the-way topics and obscure philosophies is freely admitted.

If she was a fraud, why was she such a fool to invent imaginary Teachers? Why should she make them the fathers of her knowledge, and so become a target for abuse and slander, while she might have gained esteem, to say nothing of money, by the simple and easier course of taking the entire credit herself?

Can anything more preposterous be imagined than for a Russian woman of noble family, married to a high official, go out into the world on a wild goose-chase after imaginary Teachers, and having acquired an immense mass of recondite knowledge at great cost and suffering, to throw away the credit of acquiring it, to ascribe it to nonexistent persons, to face slander, abuse and calumny instead of utilizing it in the common way, to be poor and despised when she might have been wealthy and honored?

Looked at from any standpoint consistent with reason, the only tenable conclusion is that H.P.B. told the truth when she affirmed that her knowledge was received through the Masters of Wisdom.

A curious fact in connection with images of books as seen in the astral light is that the text sometimes appears reversed as if held before a mirror. With a little practice it becomes easy to read words, as the context and general sense prevent mistakes, but reading figures correctly is more difficult.

Sometimes Madame Blavatsky forgot to reverse them, causing much trouble and annoyance to herself and others. For example, if she wrote to a friend asking him to verify a passage on page 341 of a certain book, the answer might come back that the passage could not be found there, or that there were not that many pages in the book.

Looking the matter up it was invariably found in such cases that H.P.B. had forgotten to reverse the number. So (to take the same instance) it should have been 143 instead of 341. After a time, her correspondents discovered this, and then easily corrected such mistakes themselves.

Another noteworthy circumstance in connection with the writing of *"The Secret Doctrine"* was that if Madame Blavatsky ever wanted definite information on any subject, it was sure to reach her in some way, either in a letter from a friend, in a newspaper or a magazine, or in the course of casual reading of books. This happened with such frequency and appositeness that it could not be explained on the basis of coincidence. Whenever possible, she used normal means, so as not to exhaust her powers. In the early days of the Society, she had not been prudent in this, and afterward she felt the effects.

One day there came a temptation in the offer of a large yearly salary if she would write for the Russian newspapers. She might write on any subject she chose, occultism included. Here was a primise of comfort and ease for the remainder of her days. Two hours a day would be ample to satisfy all demands on her time. But she said, *"To write such a work as `The Secret Doctrine', I must have all my thoughts in that direction, to keep in touch with the current. It is difficult enought as it is, hampered as I am with this sick and worn out old body, and it would be impossible to change the current back and forth from "The Secret Doctrine" to newspaper writing. I have no longer the energy left in me.*

Too much of it was exhausted in performing phenomena." When asked why she did these things when she must have known that she was wasting her strength and it would have been much better if no phenomena had been connected with her work, she answered, *"Because people were continually bothering me. It was always, `Oh, do materialize this,' or ' Do `let me hear those astral bells' and so on, and then I did not like to disappoint people, so I acceded to their requests. Now*

I have to suffer for it, and moreover, at the time the Society was started it was necessary to draw people's attention, and phenomena did this more effectually than anything else could have done."

Granted, then, that phenomena *were* necessary at that time, the mischief lay in the fact that, once introduced, they were difficult to get rid of when they had served their purpose. All came eager to have their curiosity gratified, and if disappointed, went away in great wrath and indignation, ready to denounce the thing as a fraud. So in her anxiety for the welfare of the Society, poor H.P.B. continued the work, knowing that she was squandering her vitality. Thus she almost literally gave her life blood for the good of the organization.

After the Society was fairly well established came the opportunity to have ease and comfort for the rest of her days. Can we realize what that meant? Picture Madame Blavatsky in her dingy little apartment with but one bedroom, which she shared with the Countess Wachmeister. In that obscure old German town she was virtually an exile among a foreign and unfamiliar people.

Here she toiled at her desk twelve to fourteen hours a day, and was often in the most straitened circumstances. Then came the offer from the newspaper. She could write about anything she pleased, and receive a salary that would place her far beyond the pale of want--all for about two hours a day of her time. Seemingly it would involve only a small sacrifice of time; but H.P.B. knew better. She knew that she could not write for newspapers and write *"The Secret Doctrine"* also. Unflinchingly she wrote the letter declining the offer, and thus added another to the long list sacrifices she had already laid on the altar of the Society and of humanity.

From Wurzburg, Madame Blavatsky went to Elberfield, where she stayed with Madame Gebhard. Here it seems that little if any work was done on "The Secret Doctrine", owing to the fact that she fell and sprained her ankle. Her kind friends nursed her tenderly, but recovery seemed to be slow. Her sister and niece were sent for, and with them she went to Ostend, from which place she wrote to the Countess Wachmeister:

"Yes, I will try to settle once more at my `Secret Doctrine' but it is hard. I am very weak. I feel I am ungrateful. But then gratitude has ever been shown in ancient symbology to reside in people's heels, and having lost my legs how can I be expected to have any?" Later she wrote: *"My poor legs have parted company with my body. I am now as legless as any elemental can be, and I do not know a soul in Ostend; not a solitary Russian here but myself, who would rather be a Turk and go back to India, but I can't, for I have neither legs nor reputation, according to the infamous charges of the S.P.R."* [* The Society for Psychical Research]

Soon afterwards, the Countess Wachmeister again joined H.P.B. They had a number of visitors from England, Germany, and France, Ostend being easy of access from these countries. Madame Blavatsky wrote steadily, though her health was very poor and she frequently fretted, as evidenced by the following extract from one of her letters in which she says, *"Because lies, hypocrisy and jesuitism reign supreme in this world, and I am not and cannot be either, therefore I seem doomed. Because I am tired of life and the struggle with that Stone of Sisyphus and the eternal work of the Danaides, and I am not permitted to get out of this misery and rest because I am one too many on this earth, I am doomed."*

This state of mind was probably occasioned chiefly by the extremely poor health which soon after came to a crisis, when she was stricken with kidney trouble. The Belgian physician said that she could not live long, and in her despair the Countess telegraphed to Dr. Ashton Ellis, one of the London members of the Theosophical Society, who immediately came to Ostend. He held out no more hope than the Belgian doctor. Both were agreed that they had never known a person with kidneys so severely affected to live so long.

It seemed as if *"The Secret Doctrine"* would not be finished--at least not by H.P.B. Anxious and sorrowful were the hearts of those who surrounded her. The grief of the Countess Wachmeister became so great that she went into a swoon. She recovered, and continued to be almost constantly at the bedside of the sick woman. Awakening one morning after a short sleep, she was surprised to see Madame Blavatsky sitting up in bed, looking calmly at her.

"Countess, come here!"

The Countess obeyed, asking: *"What is the matter, H.P.B.? You look so different."*

She replied, *"Yes. Master has been here. He gave me my choice--that I might die and be free if I would, or live and finish "The Secret Doctrine". He told me how great would be my sufferings, and what a terrible time I would have before me in England (for I am to go there) but when I thought of those to whom I shall be permitted to teach a few things and of the T.S., to which I have given my heart's blood already, I accepted the sacrifice."*

She then called for some breakfast and to the surprise and joy of her friends, got up and went into the dining-room, where later she received a lawyer and the American Consul, who had come to superintend the making of her will. One may imagine the change of expression which came over their faces when, instead of coming into the presence of a dying woman, they found Madame Blavatsky sitting in her armchair seemingly in the best of health. Thus once more the specter of death was thrust away and H.P.B. had taken another lease on life.

The next visitors were Dr. Keightley and Mr. Bertram Keightley of London, who bore urgent invitations to Madame Blavatsky to come to London. To this she finally consented. The Countess left Ostend for Sweden, and shortly H.P.B. journeyed to London, where with the Keightleys she occupied a small cottage called Maycot.

Here the manuscript of *"The Secret Doctrine"* was finished. It made a pile three feet high when it was given to the Keightleys for correction of syntax, punctuation, and spelling. The Keightleys found that it was not written in a consecutive manner, and outlined a plan of rearrangement which was approved by Madame Blavatsky. The entire manuscript was then typewritten.

Just before this work was finished, H.P.B. and her friends moved to 17 Lansdowne Road, Notting Hill, London, where they were joined by the Countess Wachmeister and others, and there was established the first Headquarters.

It was first arranged to have *"The Secret Doctrine"* published by Mr. George Redway, who was publishing *"Lucifer"*, the magazine which had been founded a short time before by H.P.B., and which has since been called the *"Theosophical Review"*, but as his proposal was not financially satisfactory, and a friend of Madame Blavatsky's offered to furnish the money, an office was taken in Duke Street, London, the primary object being to enable the Theosophical Society to derive the utmost benefit from her writings.

Of the further history of the writing of *"The Secret Doctrine"* there is little to be said, though several months more of hard work were necessary before it was finally ready for the press. H.P.B. read and corrected two sets of galley proof, then a set of page proof and finally a revise in sheet correcting, altering and adding until the last, with the result that the printers' bill for corrections alone amounted to $1,500.

Such is the story of *"The Secret Doctrine"*--a story which, like the book itself, is derided by the majority of people, notwithstanding its authentication by many persons of sound reason and blameless life. As in the case of Copernicus and others, some day the world will wake up and find that this much abused woman was right.

Will a monument be raised to her? Who knows? Whether it will be or not, the fact remains that in *"The Secret Doctrine"* itself and in the affection with which its author is regarded by every student who has been helped by her is a monument more lasting than marble or bronze.

For, though the Masters were the actual authors of the work, let us not forget that it was the zeal and devotion of H.P.B. which so excellently qualified her as an instrument for their use; and but for that zeal and devotion we might not today possess the greatest of modern works on occultism--*"The Secret Doctrine"*.

CHAPTER IV

We have traced the history of *"The Secret Doctrine"*, from the time when H.P.B.'s Master gave her the plan, until it was printed and given to the world. Now study the plan upon which it was constructed, and try to catch a glimpse of the teachings contained within its several volumes.

When we contemplate the range of subjects dealt with in this work--a range bounded only by the universe--it is at once apparent how fragmentary must be any outline. The content of *"The Secret Doctrine"* cannot be taught in one lecture not in a hundred lectures, even though such a lecture course were given by the most learned exponent.

The work is a mine rich in priceless gems of occult knowledge. Perseverance and intuition are the pick and shovel by the diligent use of which we may become possessed of these jewels of great price.

A truth discovered by ourselves stays with us after we have lost a dozen other truths explained to us by others. If therefore we can be induced to dig within *"The Secret Doctrine"* for ourselves, we shall profit more than if someone were to explain to us every teaching contained within its covers.

A cursory reading will prove a potent emans of bewildering the mind, as before us whirl demons and devas, Dhyan Chohans and Kumaras, yugas and cycles, satyrs and fakirs, adepts and alchemists, Manus and monads, in a continuous phantasmagoria.

To be of value *"The Secret Doctrine"* must be studied. Just as Theseus, who entered the labyrinth of Crete to do battle with the Minotaur, was gudied out of the maze by the thread of Ariadne, so the student should fix his mind on one subject, and plunge boldly into the maze to do battle with the Minotaur of ignorance.

If he persists, and holds tight the golden thread of intuition, he will be sure to bring out the priceless gem of knowledge of the subject; and by his toil he will have made it part of himself--a possession never to be lost. In this way he may spend days in search of a small point, but when he understands that point, he will know thsat the time was well spent.

When at last he has extracted as far as he is able the information contained in *"The Secret Doctrine"*, there dawns upon his mind a conception of the truth. I cannot describe the exultation I felt at that first view of that truth, and how I meditated on it and admired it as I saw it dovetail into all the general philosophies.

It should be remembered that the work which we are considering is not by any means the whole of the esoteric philosophy possessed by the Masters of Wisdom, but only a small fragment of its fundamental tenets. The teachings of *"The Secret Doctrine"*, however fragmentary and incomplete, do not belong to the Hindu, Zoroastrian, Chaldean, or Egyptian religions; nor to Buddhism, Islamism, Judaism or Christianity exclusively.

The book contains the essence of them all. Originating from the same source, all are in these volumes resolved into their original elements, out of which every mystery and dogma has developed and become materialized.

The aim of the work is to show that Nature is not a fortuitous concurrence of atoms, to assign to man his rightful place in the scheme of the universe, to rescue from degradation the archaic truths which are the basis of all religions, to uncover to some extent the fundamental unity from which they all sprang, and finally to show that the occult side of Nature has never been approached by the science of modern civilization.

When an architect starts to build a modern skyscraper he first prepares a solid foundation; upon this he rears the massive steel beams to form the skeleton of the building.

This skeleton is then clothed in walls and floors of concrete, terra cotta, and other materials. A system of steam-pipes like arteries carries heat to every room. Its nervous system is an intricate network of electric light and telephone wires, while in the basement throbs a steam engine, driving an electric generator. The result is an organic whole pulsing with life.

Somewhat similar was the procedure of the Masters of Wisdom who built the monumetal structure of occult knowledge which we are considering.

A Mohammedan writer says, *"In the assembly of the day of resurrection the sins of Kabak will be forgiven for the sake of the Lust of the Christian Churches."* Professor Max Muller replied, *"The sins of Islam are as worthless as the dust of Christianity. In the day of the resurrection both Christians and Mohammedans will see the vanity of their religious doctrines.*

Men fight about religion on earth. In heaven they shall find out that there only one true religion." In other words, ***"There is no religion higher than truth."*** Upon this foundation of truth was raised by the Masters of the Wisdom of the Ages the skeleton structure of the

"Book of Dzyan", a Senzar manuscript of vast antiquity, about which have been gathered all that was good and true in all the world religions, cemented by occult knowledge, and ornamented with old symbols and myths.

These were the more beautiful for being deprived of the scale of materialism which for ages had covered them. The result is the congeries of transcendent philosophy contained in *"The Secret Doctrine"*.

It may be asked: where are the arteries of steam pipes, the nervous system of electric wires, the steam engine, and the electric generator to vitalize the building? These the student must himself supply by making it part of himself, by taking it into his own life. In proportion as he does this will be the life it has for him, its measure and its limit being his devotion to its ideals.

"The Secret Doctrine" establishes three fundamental postulates. The first is the existence of an omnipresent, eternal, boundless and immutable Principle on which all specualtion is impossible, since it transcends the power of human conception and can only be dwarfed by any human expression or similitude. It is beyond the range of thought, unspeakable and unthinkable.

This Be-ness is symbolized in *"The Secret Doctrine"* under two aspects: on the one hand is Absolute Abstract Space, representing base subjectivity--the one thing which no human mind can either exclude from any conception or conceive of by itself.

On the other hand is Absolute Abstract Motive, representing unconditional consciousness. This latter aspect is also spoken of as the Great Breath, the One Reality. The Absolute is the field of absolute consciousness, or that essence which is out of all relation to conditioned existence, and of which conscious existence is a conditioned symbol; but once we pass in thought from this absolute negation (to us), duality supervenes in the contrast of Spirit (or Consciousness) and Matter.

Spirit and Matter are to be regarded not as independent realities, but as symbols or aspects of the Absolute, which constitute the basis of conditioned being, whether subjective or objective.

Considering this metaphysical triad as the root from which proceeds all manifestation, the Great Breath assumes the character of precosmic ideation. It is the fount of force and of all individual consciousness, and supplies the guiding Intelligence in the vast scheme of cosmic evolution. On the other hand, precosmic root substance is the aspect of the Absolute which underlies all the objective planes of nature.

The manifested universe is pervaded by duality, which is the very essence of its existence as Manifestation. But just as the opposite poles of subject and object, spirit and matter, are but aspects of the One Unity in which they are synthesized, so in the manifested universe there is that which links spirit to matter, subject to object.

This something--at present unknown to Western speculation--is called by Eastern occultists "fohat". It is the "bridge" by which ideas existing in the divine thought are impressed on cosmic substance.

Thus from spirit or cosmic ideation comes our consciousness; from cosmic substance come the several vehicles in which that consciousness is individualized; while this substance in its various manifestations is the mysterious link between mind and matter, the principle vivifying every atom.

The second fundamental postulate of *"The Secret Doctrine"* is the existence of eternity *in toto* as a boundless plane--periodically the playground of numberless universes which are incessantly manifesting and disappearing.

This postulate is the absolute universality of that law of periodicity, of flux and reflux, ebb and flow, which physical science has observed and recorded in all departments of nature. An alternation such as that of day and night, waking and sleeping, life and death, is in fact so common, so perfectly universal and without exception, that it is easy to see in it one of the fundamental laws of the universe.

The third and last of the basic postulates of *"The Secret Doctrine"* is the fundamental identity of all souls with the universal Oversoul, the latter being itself an aspect of the Unknown Root; and the obligatory pilgrimage of every soul through a cycle of incarnation. These souls or sparks are the Sons abiding from everlasting, from the beginning of the creative age in the bosom of the Father.

They are to be made perfect through sufferings. Each soul is truly equal to the Father as concerns its Godhead, but inferior to the Father as concerns its manhood, and each is to go forth into matter in order to render all things subject to itself. The soul is to be sown in weakness that it may be raised in power, thus escaping from the limitations of a static Logos, enfolding all divine powers, ominiscient and ominpresent on its own plane, but unconscious on all other planes.

Its glory is to be veiled in soul-blinding matter in order that through experience, the soul may become omnisicent and omnipresent ON ALL PLANES, repsonsive to all divine vibrations instead of to those on the highest planes only. The pivotal doctrine of the hidden wisdom admits of no privileges or special gifts in man save those won by his own soul through a long series of metempsychoses and reincarnations.

Such are the basic conceptions on which *"The Secret Doctrine"* rests. It would not be fitting here to enter upon any defense or proof of their inherent reasonableness, nor can I pause to show how they are contained--though too often under a misleading guise--in all systems of thought or philosophy worthy of the name. Once the student has gained a clear comprehension of them and realized the light they throw on every problem of life, he finds that they need no further justification.

The history of cosmic evolution as traced in the *Stanzas of Dzyan* may be regarded as the abstract algebraic formula of that evolution.

Hence the student must not expect to find there an account of all the stages ands transformations which have occurred between the beginnings of universal evolution and our present state. To give such an account would be as impossible as it would be incomprehensible to men who cannot grasp the nature of even the plane of existence next to their own.

The Stanzas, therefore, give an abstract formula which can be applied to all evolution--to that of our tiny earth, to the chain of planets of which our earth forms one, to the solar universe to which that chain belongs, and so on, in an ascending scale until the mind reels an is exhausted in the effort to understand.

The seven Stanzas of the first volume represent the seven terms of the abstract formula to which they refer, and describe the seven great stages of the evolutionary process mentioned in the Hindu philosophy as the seven creations, and in the Bible as the days of creation.

Stanza No. 1: describes the condition of the Absolute One during the interlude between cosmic manifestations and before the first flutter of reawakening activity. A moment's consideration will show how difficult it is to describe such a state. Since it is a state of Absoluteness per se, it can possess none of the specific attributes which serve to describe objects in positive terms.

Hence the state can be suggested only by negatives involving all the most abstract attributes which men feel rather than conceive as the remotest limits attainable by their powers of conception. We are informed by the Stanza that:

Stanza No. 1: *"The eternal parent wrapped in her ever invisible robes had slumbered once again for seven eternities. Time was not, for it lay asleep in the infinite bosom of duration. Universal mind was not, for there were no Ah-Hi to contain it. The seven ways to bliss were not. The great causes of misery were not, for there was no one to produce and get ensnared by them. Darkness alone filled the boundless all, for father, mother and son were once more one, and the son had not awakened yet for the new wheel, and his pilgrimage thereon.*

The seven sublime lords and the seven truths had ceased to be, and the Universe, the son of Necessity, was immersed in Paranishpanna [the Absolute], to be outbreathed by that which is and yet is not. Naught was. The causes of existence had been done away with; the visible that was, and the invisible that is, rested in eternal non-being--the one being. Alone the one form of existence stretched boundless, infinite, causeless, in dreamless sleep; and life pulsated un-

conscious in universal space, throughout that All-presence which is sensed by the opened eye of the Dangma [the inner spiritual eye of the seer, or the Third Eye]."

Stanza No. 2: describes a stage which to the Western Mind is so nearly identical with the first that to explain the difference would require a treatise in itself. A grasp of what it contains can be obtained only through the intuition and higher faculties of the student. Indeed, it must be remembered that all the Stanzas appeal more to the inner faculties than to the physical brain:

*"Where were the Builders, the luminous Sons of Manvantaric Dawn? * * * The producers of form from no-form--the root of the world--? * * Where was silence? Where the ears to sense it? No, there was neither silence nor sound; naught save ceaseless eternal breath, which knows itself not. The hour had not yet struck; the ray had not yet flashed into the Germ; the Matripadma [Mother- Lotus] had not yet swollen. * * * The universe was still concelaed in the Divine thought and the Divine bosom."*

Stanza No. 3: describes the reawakening of the universe to activity after rest. It depicts the emergence of the monads from their state of absorption within the One. Thus begins the earliest and highest stage in the formation of worlds. The term "monad" may apply to the vastest solar system and the tiniest atom. Says the Stanza:

"The last vibration of the seventh eternity thrills through inifinitude. The mother swells, expanding from within without, like thge bud of the lotus. The vibration sweeps along, touching with its swift wing the whole universe and the germ that dwelleth in darkness. The darkness that breathes over the [slum-

bering waters of life. Darkness radiates light, and light drops one solitary ray into the mother-deep.

*The ray shoots through the virgin egg, the ray causes the virgin egg to thrill, and drop the non-eternal germ, which condenses into the world-egg. * * * Father-Mother spin a web whose upper end is fastened to spirit--the light of the one darkness--and the lower one to its shadowy end, matter; and this web is the universe spun out of the two wubstances made in one. * * * It expands when the breath of fire is upon it; it contracts when the breath of the mother touches it. Then the sons dissociate and scatter, to return into their mother's bosom at the end of the great day, and re-become one with her: * * *"*

Stanza No. 4: shows the differentiation of the germ of the universe into the septenary hierarchy of conscious Divine Power which is the active manifestation of the one supreme energy. They are the framers, shapers, and ultimately the creators of all the manifested universe in the only sense in which the name Creator is intelligible. They inform and guide it.

They are intelligent beings who adjust and control evolution, embodying in themselves those manifestations of the one Law which we know as the Law of Nature. This stage of evolution is called in mythology the Creation of the Gods, but it is [PAGE 202] not a creation of gods in the sense in which creation is generally understood in the West, but as a reawakening into activity of Beings who have acquired their transcendental intelligences in former universes.

Stanza No. 5: *"The Primordial Seven, the First Seven Breaths of the Dragon of Wisdom, produce in their turn from their Holy Circumgyrating Breaths the Fiery Whirlwind."*

The stanza describes the process of world formation; first, diffused cosmic matter, then the fiery whirlwind--the first stage in the formation of a nebula. This nebula condenses, and after passing through various transformations froms a solar universe, a planetary chain, or a single planet, as the case may be.

Stanza No. 6: indicates the subsequent stages in the formation of such a world, and brings its evolution down to the fourth period--corresponding to the period in which we are now living.

" * * He builds them in the likeness of older wheels, placing them on the Imperishable Centres. How does Fohat build them? He collects the fiery dust. He makes balls of fire, runs through them, and round them, infusing life thereinto, then sets them into motion; some one way, some the other way. They are cold, he makes them hot. They are dry, he makes them moist. They shine, he fans and cools them. Thus acts Fohat from one twilight to the other, during Seven Eternities. * * * Make thy calculations, Lanoo, if thou wouldest learn the correct age of the small wheel. Its fourth spoke is our mother. Reach the fourth "fruit" of the fourth path of knowlkedge that leads to Nirvana, and thou shalt comprehend, for thou shalt see."*

*Stanza No. 7: "Behold the beginning of sentient formless life. * * * The one ray multiplies the smaller rays. Life precedes form, and life survives the last atom of form. Through the countless rays proceeds the life-ray, the One, like a thread through many jewels. * * * The spark hangs from the flame by the finest thread of Fohat. It journeys through the Seven World of Maya. It stops in the first, and is a metal and a stone; it passes into the second and behold--a plant; the plant whirls through seven changes and becomes* *a sacred animal. From the combines atteibutes of these, Manu, the thinker is formed.*

The 7th Stanza continues the history, tracing the descent of life down to the appearance of man, thus ending the description of comsic evoltuion as found in the first volume.

For a graphic summary of the teaching of "The Secret Doctrine" on the cosmogony of the system of worlds to which we belong, it would be difficult to improve upon that given in an old commentary on the ***Book of Dzyan.*** *"Eight houses were built by Mother [Space]. Eight houses for her Eight Divine sons [planets]; four large and four small ones. Eight brilliant suns, according to their age and merits. Bal-i-lu (Marrtanda) [the eighth sun, the sun of our solar system] was not satisfied, though his house was the largest. He began (to work) as the huge elephants do. He breathed (drew in) into his timach the vital airs of his brothers. He sought to devour them.*

The larger four were far away; far, on the margin of their kingdom (planetary system). They were not robbed (affected) and laughed. Do your worst, Sir, you cannot reach us, they said. But the smaller wept. They complained to the Mother. She exiled Bal-i-lu to the center of her Kingdom, from whence he could not move. (Since then) he (only) watches and threatens. He pursues them, turning slowly around himself, they turning swiftly from him, and he following from afar the direction in which his brothers move on the path that encircles their houses. (`The sun rotates on his axis always in the same direction in which the planets revolve in their respective orbits.' astronomy teaches us)."

If there is anywhere a plainer and more graphic exposition I should like to know it. Modern astronomy also explains this phenomenon, though in some points it differs. The occult doctrine rejects the hypothesis (born of the nebular theory) that the seven great planets have evolved from the central mass of the sun--at least, of our visible sun.

The first condensation of cosmic matter took place around a central nucleus, its parent sun, but according to the occult teaching, the sun merely detached itself earlier than the others, as the rotating mass contracted, and is their elder brother and not their father.

Each of these seven planets in its turn is again associated with six other planets. Such a group is called a planetary chain. Each of these chains froms a field of evolution for a certain number of monads or souls. There are further subdivisions, but we need not be concerned with them here.

Evolution of these monads progresses through a series of manifestations on one or more of these chains, and, just as this earth is the fourth and most material planet of the seven globes which are the field of its special system of evolution, do does this whole chain of worlds occupy the same place in the larger scheme to which it belongs; that is to say, the life impulse which is now cycling through this present period of evolution had its beginning long anterior to it.

There have been three such periods of evolution before this one, and there will be three after this one has passed, before objective manifestation once more returns to the bosom of the Infinite for a period of rest.

Our own little earth and its human inhabitants are given due consideration in the second volume of *"The Secret Doctrine"*. To understand it is by no means the simple task which one might suppose when viewing the pictures representing the creation story in some of the old cathedrals of Europe, where God appears much as a Nuremburg toymaker, hanging the planets in the firmament, or sitting cross-legged on a table with a large pair of scissors beside him, sewing coats of skin for Adam and Eve.

We understand also that the geological constitution of the earth cannot be accounted for by the six-day or any other creation theory, for if God created the world as thus set forth, we must also suppose that he twisted the strata, stored the fossils between, scooped out the valleys supposed to have been made by glaciers, and caused the marks of erosion by water all for His own glory and for the mystification of man.

"The Secret Doctrine" teaches that the fire-mist which eventually condensed into what is now our earth originally covered an area so large that it enveloped the moon. The latter was heated to such an extent that it was softened to the consistency of mud; its water and air were converted into steam, and when the fire-mist contracted, the atmosphere and water followed the new center.

When the earth had cooled sufficiently, the enveloping fire-mist condensed into our present water and air, until at the time when the life-wave reached the earth from Mars in the course of the present round, the earth had cooled so much that the water had become tepid. About this time, the first of the four great continents--which existed before the earth assumed its present topography--appeared in the region now known as the Arctic.

CHAPTER V

Before going any further, it is necessary to understand the central position of our earth in the whole plan of evolution. During the preceding three and one-half rounds, the monads have been veiling themselves more and more in matter. On the earth in our present round, the nadir of materiality was reached by all kingdoms in the middle of the fourth race.

We, being in the fifth sub-race of the firth root-race, are just beginning to slowly raise ourselves out of matter. We are the prodigal sons who went into a far country to gather experience, and having gone as afr as we could, are now returning home to our Father--who be the pouring out of Intelligence has met us a long way off, and is now conducting us to our own spiritual home.

 The general plan of human evolution on the globe is briefly this: seven distinct root-races were destined to evolve a certain principle or sense. In this way, the four races which preceded us developed hearing, touch, sight, and taste.

We have developed smell. The sixth and seventh root-races are to develop astral and mental clairvoyance respectively. They will also develop spirituality. We are developing intellectuality; our predecessors developed desire. Each of the seven root-races divides into seven sub-races, these again being subdivided. The evolution of each root-race takes place under the guidance of a special teacher, a great spiritual entity who incarnates in that race as ruler and lawgiver.

Each root-race evolves on its own continent, which is destroyed when that evolution is finished, water and fire being used alternately as agents. The archaic names of these continents are many, but to avoid confusion *"The Secret Doctrine"* uses the names most familiar to Western readers.

The first continent it calls the Imperishable Sacred Land. The reason for this name is that this continent is the only one whose destiny it is to last throughout the whole of our stay on this chain of globes. It was the cradle of the first man, and will be the dwelling of the last divine mortal Chaya as a repository for the future seeds of humanity.

This sacred land has in its center Mount Meru, whose roots are in the Himalayan chain; from the peak of this sacred mountain--which forms the axis of the earth--there is a continuous flow of magnetic current, whcih spreads over the whole globe, re-entering it at the south pole.

Thence it goes to the Holy City of Shamballah (the heart of the earth) in the Gobi Desert, where it is purified by the Masters of the Great White Lodge, and sent back to Mount Meru at the north pole. Around the sacred mountain, like leaves of the lotus, are seven promontories. On these were born the seven sub-classes of the first race, says the *"Book of Dzyan"*:
"The great Chohans [Lords] called the Lords of the Moon, of the Airy Bodies. `Bring forth men, men of your nature. Give them their forms within. She will build coverings without. Males- females will they be.'
* * * They [the Moon-gods] went each on his allotted land: seven of them each on his lot."

Concerning anthropogenesis, "The Secret Doctrine" teaches:

(1) the simultaneous evolution of seven human groups on seven different portions of our globe;

(2) the birth of the astral bdoy before the physical, the latter body being molded in the astral form;

(3) the priority of man in this round to the animals, the monkeys included. This last teaching is in accord with the second creation story in the Bible; also with other books.

On the Sacred Imperishable Land were created by the Lords of the Moon chain the first race--large, shadowy, ethereal beings floating hither and thither. It may be asked, why call them human?

For the same reason that a human fetus is called human, when for the first eight weeks it si indistinguishable from the embryonic dog. The method by which these beings reproduced was to throw off their astral counterpart, which in time could throw off another, each inferior to his father. This provides the explanation of the varying stages of humanity, for such inferior beings were ensouled by enferior entities.

This race did not die, but was clother with the second race. The latter, after the type had been definitely established, was led to what *"The Secret Doctrine"* calls the Hyperborean continent, the promontories of which stretched from the North Pole to the south and west. In the days of Homer the Greeks spoke of it as a blessed land beyond the reach of Boreas, the god of winter, and of the hurricane--an ideal country, where nights were short and days were long.

On this continent lived the second-race men, ensouled by the second great host of monads which had come over from the Moon chain. Although having the general form of men, the individuals of this race were gigantic jellylike creatures who floated over the surface of the earth, as directed by passing desires.

The features were undefined, there being no eyes, ears, or mouth. They received impressions through and were guided by two centers of force, the so-called thrid eye (which has become the pineal gland) and an organ which has developed into the spleen. They were potentially bisexual, and reproduced their species in the same manner as the first race. The second-race men were boneless--which accounts for the fact that geologists have found no fossils in the three lower strata.

During the later secondary period the waters receded, and land appeared in the areas now covered by India, China, Australia, Africa, the Pacific Ocean and Northern Europe. This was the vast Lemurian continent, to which the great Lemurian race was led by its Teacher. This was the first race to receive the outpouring of intelligence.

The mode of reproduction was changed three times during this period. Says the **"Book of Dzyan": "Then the second [race] evolved the Egg-born, the third. * * * The egg of the future race, the Man-swan of the later third. First male-female, then man and woman."** Today embryology teaches that man is born from the ovum; that in the third month the fetus is bisexual; then one sexual organ becomes dominant, the other remaining rudimentary but never disappearing.

The body of the third root race man became firmer, and its shape changed until it was man as we know he was--a giant twelve to fifteen feet tall, with a dark yellow-brown skin, long lower jaw, flat face, eyes far apart, the head sloping upward and backward.

He had no forehead; the hair was short, the back of the head bare, probably for the greater convenience of the third eye. Arms and legs were much longer in proportion than ours. His heels projected back, so that he could walk backward. Certainly he was not too engaging a person. We can sympathize with the souls who were guided to such bodies for incarnation, and excuse them for refusing.

During this age the animals appeared, and separated into sexes before man. Up to this stage, man had remained (as the *"Book of Dzyan"* puts it) **"an empty, senseless shadow."** Then came the time when he was to receive the priceless gift of mind. To accomplish this three classes of souls came down to birth.

The first were the Lords of Venus, who, though not belonging to our planetary chain, sent to this earth-- their adopted child--great teachers who taught and guided infant humanity. To them we can give thanks for the fact that we are now about one round in advance of what we otherwise would have achieved.

These Lords established the Great White Lodge, which has existed ever since, and from which have been sent all the great Teachers of humanity. Originally the Lodge was not for the benefit of evolving humanity-- which for ages was not to be qualified to tread the path of initiation--but for those of the Lords of Venus who had not reached the highest stage of initiation.

The other two classes are described as the Sons of Wisdom and the Sons of Night. Of these the Sons of Night refused to create. Those who entered became sages; on those who did not procreate, the curse was pronounced. They will be born in the fourth suffering, and causing suffering.

Thus was a part of humanity left narrow-headed and mindless. Of them the *"Book of Dzyan"* says: **"And those which had no spark took huge she-animals unto them. They begat upon them dumb races. Dumb they were themselves. But their tongues untied. The tongues of their progeny remained still. Monsters they bred. A race of crooked red-hair-covered monsters going on all fours. A dumb race to keep the shame untold. Seeing which, the Lhas [the spirits, the Sons of Wisdom] who had not built men, wept, saying: `The Amanasa [the mindless] have defiled our future abodes. This is Karma [retribution]. Let us dwell in the other. Let us teach them better, lest worse should happen. * * * Then all men become endowed with Manas [mind]."**

Some of the fourth race men who had mind, however, did the same--and here is the explanation of *"The Secret Doctrine"* regarding the anthropoids. They are not our ancestors--as is assumed by the evolutionists--but an offshoot of the human race. They are the only animals now on the globe which will develop human astral forms in the seventh root-race, and will be definitely human in the fifth round.

There is still another class, of which one division incarnated during thr later third and the other during the early fourth round. They had advanced too far on the Lunar chain to be reborn on the earthly chain during the preceding stages, and came into incarnation for the first time on this chain. These are the last of the monads who inhabited the Moon chain.

From the seventh sub-race of the third race the Teacher who was to develop the coming fourth race singled out those who were to form the nucleus, and led them to that great see-ground for humanity--the Imperishable Sacred Land-- where he segregated them, says the *"Book of Dzyan"*, two by two, on the seven zones, and imbedded in their forms potentially the qualities to be developed in the coming races.

Meanwhile great cataclysms rent the continent, and Lemuria as such disappeared, ages before the tertiary period. In its place rose Atlantis, the fourth continent, destined to become the seat of a civilization which in many ways excelled our own. Its rulers were divine Priest-Kings. It was indeed the Golden Age; alchemistry was used to produce gold for use in the arts and to ornament their houses and buildings. Superphysical powers were a common possession.

When the divine pilots tried the experiment of relinquishing the helm to see if man himself would be able to guide the ship of humanity, this was all changed. *"Then the Fourth [race] became tall with pride. We are the kings, it was said; we are the gods. They took wives fair to look upon. Wives from the mindless, the narrow-headed. They bred monsters. Wicked demons, male and female. * * They built temples for the human body. Male and female they worshipped. Then the Third Eye acted no longer.*

*They built huge cities. * * * They built great images nine yatis high, the size of their bodies. Inner fires had destroyed the land of their fathers. The water threatened the fourth. The first great waters came. They swallowed the seven great islands."* Such is the Story of the degradation into which fell the class which the BOOK calls the Lords of Night, or the Dark Faces, in contradistinction to the Sons of Wisdom, or Lords of the Dazzling Face. *"The Secret Doctrine"* tells the story plainly:

"And the `great King of the Dazzling Face', the chief of all the Yellow- faced, seeing the sins of the Black-faced, was sad. He sent his air-vehicles to all his brothers-chiefs (chiefs of other nations and tribes) with pious men within saying `Prepare, arise ye men of the good law, and cross the land while (yet) dry. The Lords of the storm are approaching. Their chariots are nearing the land. One night and two days only shall the Lords of the Dark Face (the Sorcerers) live on this patient land. She is doomed, and they have to descend with her.

The nether Lords of the Fires (the Gnomes and fire Elemntals) are preparing their magic Agneyastra (fire-weapons worked by magic). * * * They are versed in Ashtar (Vidya, the highest magical [PAGE 216] knowledge). Come and use yours (your magic powers, in order to counteract those of the Sorcerers). Let every lord of the Dazzling Face (and adept of the White Magic) cause the Viwan of every lord of the Dark Face to come into his hands (or possession), lest any (of the Sorcerers) should by its means escape from the waters, avoid the rod of the Four, (Karmic deities) and save his wicked (followers or people). May every yellow face send sleep from himself (mesmerize?) to every black face.

May even they (the Sorcerers) avoid pain and suffering. May every man true to the Solar Gods bind (paralyze) every man under the lunar gods, lest he should suffer or escape his destiny. * * * The hour has struck, the black night is ready, etc., etc.' " The waters arose and covered the valleys from one end of the earth to the other. So perished Atlantis and came into being the story of the deluge.

From the fifth sub-race of the fourth root-race, the original Semitic, had been chosen by the Holy Vaivaswata, the Teacher of our fifth root-race, the families who were to be the ancestors of the coming race.

The Teacher led them northward to the Sacred Imperishable Land, where with loving care he instilled into them the potential characteristics of our present humanity. When ages had passed, he led them again southward to Central Asia--the land which has risen in place of the doomed Atlantis.

Already the continents had taken essentially the forms in which they now exist. From Central Asia proceeded the different migrations. The first sub-race, the Aryan, went southward to India.

The second, the Aryan Semitic, peopled Arabia and Syria. The third, the Iranian, led by Zarathustra, journeyed to Persia. The fourth, the Keltic, led by Orpheus, settled in Greece, Italy, France, Ireland, Scotland, and England. The fifth, the Teutonic, occupied Central Europe.

What does *"The Secret Doctrine"* say about the future? The land-body now known as North America will be consumed by fire. In its place will arise a new continent which will be the home of a spiritual people.

This will be the sixth root-race, the nucleus of which is being evolved right here, under the Stars and Stripes. In that race, function will be restored to the pituitary body and the pineal gland, which have been inactive since the degradation of the fourth race.

These two glands are not merely--as science says--two horny warts covered by sand, but two very important organs temporarily out of use. They are the keys to the spiritual worlds, which will in that race be opened to all mankind.

The granules with which these bodies are covered are absent in children under seven and in congenital idiots. Weak-minded people have but few.

This race will be male-female and the sympathetic nerve will develop into a second spinal cord. They will be a beautiful, spiritual and mighty people. Yet this race with its continent will also pass away, to give place to the seventh and last of our root-races.

The people of this last race will dwell on a land to the south of us, there evolving to a state transcending our present understanding. Mental clairvoyance will be possessed by all; the two spinal cords will merge into one, and man will be sexless. Then will come the time when the life-wave will once more leave our earth to conquer other worlds.

Such is the sublime plan to which we belong, as outlined in the first and second volumes of *"The Secret Doctrine"*. The third volume consists of a miscellaneous collection of papers published after the death of the author.

As the years pass, the truth of the statements in *"The Secret Doctrine"* are being gradually vindicated. As the knowledge of students grow, their admiration and reverence for their great teacher becomes more profound.

With but few and unimportant exceptions, everything which is to be found in the voluminous literature of modern occultism has been available in *"The Secret Doctrine"* ever since its publication. In the work is food for the heart and for the intellect--a system of thought and knowledge which, if we will but study it and put it into our lives, can make us wise unto salvation.

APHORISMS
FROM MAX HEINDEL'S WRITINGS

As our body is the visible garment of the invisible ego, so does the visible fire clothe the true invisible fire. Fire and the ego are both spirits and both manifest under analogous laws.

A good memory is one that forgets the faults of others, but remembers the lessons.

A small man is always anxious for a big position because he feels that the position will confer dignity and prestige upon him, but there are ninety-nine chances that he will disgrace the position. A big man dignifies any position, big or little, by the efficient way he handles it.

No matter how high that ideal seems or how far below it we feel, Saints have realized it. They were men, and what man has done man can do again.

THE LOST WORD--You cannot say it unless you have first learned to live it.

PRAYER is magic incantation, but unless your life is a prayer, you will never get the answer.

When you have set your goal, never harbor a thought of fear or failure, but cultivate an attitude of invincible determination to accomplish your object despite all obstacles, holding the thought of success constantly.

The Black Grail feeds on evil, while the Holy Grail feeds on Love. If evil did not exist the powers of darkness would starve.

Prayer is like the turning on of the electric switch, that does not create the current but simply provides a channel through which the electric current may flow. In like manner prayer creates a channel through which the divine life and light pour itself into us for our spiritual illumination.

There is but one safe way to develop our latent faculties. No matter what anyone may say to the contrary, experience will prove that attainment to spiritual powers depends upon purification and unselfish aspiration; and that is what the mysteries taught in olden times.

Nature is the symbolic expression of God. She does nothing gratuitously, but there is a purpose behind everything and every act.

It is one thing to go out in the mountains where there is no one to contradict or to jar upon our sensibilities and keep our poise; but it is another thing entirely to maintain our spiritual aspirations and keep our balance in the world where everything jars upon us; but when we stay on this path we gain a self-control which is unattainable in any other manner.

When we work and pray, and make our lives a living prayer for opportunities to serve others, then all earthly things will come of their own accord as we need them, and they will continue to come according to the degree that they are used in the service of God.

A great and wonderful allegory is written in cosmic characters in the sky. It is also written in our own lives, and warns us to forsake the fleeting life of the material and to seek the eternal life of God.

There can be no contradiction in nature, therefore the heart and mind must be capable of uniting. To indicate this common ground is precisely the purpose of this book; to show where and how the mind, helped by the intuition of the heart, can probe more deeply into the mysteries of being then either could alone, where the heart by union with the mind, can be kept from going astray, where each can have full scope for action, neither doing violence to the other, where both mind and heart can be satisfied.

The Founder of the Christian Religion stated an occult maxim when He said, **"Whosoever shall not receive the kingdom of God as a little child, he shall not enter therein."** (Mark 10). All occultists recognize the far-reaching importance of this teaching of Christ, and endeavor to live it day by day.

If, having knowledge and choice, man ranges himself on the side of good and right, he cultivates virtue and wisdom. If he succumbs to temptation and does wrong knowingly, he fosters vice.

In service is the only true greatness. Yet no matter how efficiently we may serve, if we glory in our services, that self-glory is our only reward.

It should be our aim to think little of that which we do, to esteem ourselves as nothing, for no matter how well we work, none of us are able to serve God worthily even for one single day. So HUMILITY in service should be our chief end and aim. The more thoroughly we can attain to that ideal, the smaller we are in our own eyes, the greater shall we be in the sight of God.

It is always easy to get people to do big things, where they are bolstered up by the dignity of the position. Lots of little men can always be found to fill the conspicuous places, for this man enjoys to have everybody bowing before him, but it takes a BIG MAN to do the little things, the things which are called menial, which are not menial for the personality dignifies the task.

No matter what people say to us or about us their words have no intrinsic power to hurt. It is our own mental attitude towards their utterances which determines the effect of their words upon us for good or ill. Paul, when facing persecution and slander, testified that, "None of these things moved us."

Appendix A

Max Heindel - born Carl Louis von Grasshoff in Aarhus, Denmark on July 23, 1865 - was a Christian occultist, astrologer, and mystic. He died on January 6, 1919 at Oceanside, California, United States.

Max Heindel was born of the royal family of Von Grasshoffs, who were connected with the German Court during the lifetime of Prince Bismark.

The father of Max Heindel, Francois L. von Grasshoff, migrated, when quite a young man, to Copenhagen, Denmark, where he married a Danish woman of noble birth. They had two sons and one daughter.

The oldest of these sons was Carl Louis Von Grasshoff, who later adopted the pen name of Max Heindel. The father died when the eldest son was six years of age, leaving the mother with her three small children in very straitened circumstances.

His infancy was lived in genteel poverty. His mother's self-denial was carried to an extreme in order that the small income would suffice that her sons and daughter could have private tutors so that they might take their place in society as members of nobility.

At the age of sixteen years, refusing a foreseeable future among the nobility class, he left home to enter the ship-yards at Glasgow, Scotland in order to learn the engineering profession.

He was soon chosen as Chief Engineer of a trading steamer, position which took him in trips all over the world and gave him a great deal of knowledge of the world and its people. For a number of years he was Chief Engineer on one of the large passenger steamers of the Cunard Line plying between America and Europe.

He was married, the marriage being terminated by the death of his wife in 1905. A son and two daughters were born of this marriage.

In 1903, Max Heindel moved to Los Angeles, California, in order to look for a job. Meanwhile, due to his earlier years that had been full of sorrow and to sad events in his own life, an increasingly intense desire to understand the cause of the sorrows and sufferings of humanity began to grow within him, as well as a desire to help alleviate them.

Giving a new course to his life, he became interested in the study of metaphysics and, after attending lectures by the theosophist C.W. Leadbeater, he joined the Theosophical Society of Los Angeles, of which he was vice-president in 1904 and 1905.

He also became a vegetarian and began the study of astrology, which he found to his delight gave him the key by means of which he found he could unlock the mysteries of man's inner nature.

At this time, he met Augusta Foss who was also interested along similar lines of research and in astrology; she would become his future wife. However, overwork and privation brought on him a severe heart trouble in 1905 and for months he lay at the point of death but upon recovery he was even more keenly awake to the needs of humanity.

It is said that much of the time during this illness he spent out of the body, consciously working and seeking for the truth as he might find it on the invisible planes.

From 1906 to 1907 he started a lecture tour, in order to spread his occult knowledge, in San Francisco and then in Seattle and in the northern part of the country. After a course of lectures in that city he was again forced to spend some time in a hospital with valvular heart trouble. Still undaunted, he once more took up his work of lecturing in the northwestern part of the United States.

In the fall of 1907, during a most successful period of lectures in Minnesota, he travelled to Berlin (Germany) with his friend Dr. Alma Von Brandis, who had been for months trying to persuade him, in order to hear a cycle of lectures by a teacher in the occult field called Rudolf Steiner.

During his short stay at Germany, he developed a sincere admiration by the personality of this knowledgeable lecturer, as latter shown in a dedication of his magnum opus ("esteemed teacher and value friend").

He sat in on several lectures and had one or two interviews with Steiner and he could learn about occult truth from the founder of later Anthroposophy, but at the same time he understood that this teacher had little to give to him.

It was then, with his mind already made up to return, feeling that in vain he had given up a big work in America to take this trip, that Heindel reports to have been visited by a Spiritual being (clothed in his vital body).

The highly evolved entity that visited Heindel eventually identified himself as an Elder Brother of the Rosicrucian Order, an Order in the inner worlds formed in the year 1313 and having no direct connection to physical organizations which call themselves by this name.

As he afterwards mentions, the Elder Brother gave him information which was concise and logical and beyond anything he was capable of writing. Later, he found out that during a previous visit of the Elder Brother, he was put to a test to determine his worthiness to be messenger of the Western Wisdom Teachings.

He recounts that only then he was given instruction how to reach the etheric Temple of the Rose Cross, near the German/Bohemian border, and how at this Temple he was in direct communication with and under the personal instructions of the Elder Brothers of the Rose Cross.

The Rosicrucian Order is described as being composed of twelve Elder Brothers, gathered around a thirteenth who is the invisible Head. These great Adepts, belonging to human evolution but having already advanced far beyond the cycle of rebirth, are reported as being among those exalted Beings who guide mankind's evolution, the Compassionate Ones.

Heindel returned to America in the summer of 1908 where he at once started to formulate the Rosicrucian teachings, the Western Wisdom Teachings, which he had received from the Elder Brothers, published as a book entitled The Rosicrucian Cosmo-Conception in 1909. This book became his magnum opus.

It is a reference work in the Christian mysticism practice and in the Occult study literature, containing the fundamentals of Esoteric Christianity from a Rosicrucian perspective. The Cosmo contains a comprehensive outline of the evolutionary processes of man and the universe, correlating science with religion.

Appendix B

It is said that many intelligent and otherwise capable people owned the Secret Doctrine but only a handful actually understood and comprehended it in its totality.

The problem is that the esteemed author, Madame Blavatsky used a prose and style that many contemporary readers would have trouble reading and understanding. The sheer size of the books is formidable.

In addition the Secret Doctrine attempts to cover everything from the complete Cosmology of The Universe, God and the devil – just to name a few of the subjects. The third, also called *Lost Volume* of the work was published and mostly written by her disciple Annie Bessant, who naturally knew a great deal less than her Master.

According to P.G.B. Bowen, Blavatsky gave the following instructions regarding the study of the Secret Doctrine:

"Reading the Secret .Doctrine page by page as one reads any other book (she says) will only end us in confusion. The first thing to do, even if it takes years, is to get some grasp of the "Three Fundamental Principles" given in the Proem. Follow that up by study of the Recapitulation - the numbered items in the Summing Up to Vol. I (Part 1.) Then take the Preliminary Notes (Vol. II) and the Conclusion (Vol. II)."

The Secret Doctrine establishes three fundamental propositions: --

(a) An Omnipresent, Eternal, Boundless, and Immutable **PRINCIPLE** on which all speculation is impossible, since it

transcends the power of human conception and could only be dwarfed by any human expression or similitude. It is beyond the range and reach of thought -- in the words of Mandukya, "unthinkable and unspeakable."

To render these ideas clearer to the general reader, let him set out with the postulate that there is one absolute Reality which antecedes all manifested, conditioned, being.

This Infinite and Eternal Cause -- dimly formulated in the "Unconscious" and "Unknowable" of current European philosophy -- is the rootless root of "all that was, is, or ever shall be." It is of course devoid of all attributes and is essentially without any relation to manifested, finite Being.

It is "Be-ness" rather than Being (in Sanskrit, *Sat*), and is beyond all thought or speculation.

This "Be-ness" is symbolised in the Secret Doctrine under two aspects. On the one hand, absolute abstract Space, representing bare subjectivity, the one thing which no human mind can either exclude from any conception, or conceive of by itself. On the other, absolute Abstract Motion representing Unconditioned Consciousness.

Even our Western thinkers have shown that Consciousness is inconceivable to us apart from change, and motion best symbolises change, its essential characteristic.

This latter aspect of the one Reality, is also symbolised by the term "The Great Breath," a symbol sufficiently graphic to need no further elucidation. Thus, then, the first fundamental axiom of the Secret Doctrine is this metaphysical **O**NE **A**BSOLUTE -- **BE**-NESS -- symbolised by finite intelligence as the theological Trinity.

It may, however, assist the student if a few further explanations are given here.

Herbert Spencer has of late so far modified his Agnosticism, as to assert that the nature of the "First Cause,"* which the Occultist more logically derives from the "Causeless Cause," the "Eternal," and the "Unknowable," may be essentially the same as that of the Consciousness which wells up within us: in short, that the impersonal reality pervading the Kosmos is the pure noumenon of thought. This advance on his part brings him very near to the esoteric and Vedantin tenet.*

Parabrahm (the One Reality, the Absolute) is the field of Absolute Consciousness, *i.e.,* that Essence which is out of all relation to conditioned existence, and of which conscious existence is a conditioned symbol. But once that we pass in thought from this (to us) Absolute Negation, duality supervenes in the contrast of Spirit (or consciousness) and Matter, Subject and Object.

Spirit (or Consciousness) and Matter are, however, to be regarded, not as independent realities, but as the two facets or aspects of the Absolute (Parabrahm), which constitute the basis of conditioned Being whether subjective or objective.

Considering this metaphysical triad as the Root from which proceeds all manifestation, the great Breath assumes the character of precosmic Ideation. It is the *fons et origo* of force and of all individual consciousness, and supplies the guiding intelligence in the vast scheme of cosmic Evolution. On the other hand, precosmic root-substance (*Mulaprakriti*) is that aspect of the Absolute which underlies all the objective planes of Nature.

Just as pre-Cosmic Ideation is the root of all individual consciousness, so pre-Cosmic Substance is the substratum of matter in the various grades of its differentiation.

Hence it will be apparent that the contrast of these two aspects of the Absolute is essential to the existence of the "Manifested Universe."

Apart from Cosmic Substance, Cosmic Ideation could not manifest as individual consciousness, since it is only through a vehicle** of matter that consciousness wells up as "I am I," a physical basis being necessary to focus a ray of the Universal Mind at a certain stage of complexity. Again, apart from Cosmic Ideation, Cosmic Substance would remain an empty abstraction, and no emergence of consciousness could ensue.

The "Manifested Universe," therefore, is pervaded by duality, which is, as it were, the very essence of its EX-istence as "manifestation."

But just as the opposite poles of subject and object, spirit and matter, are but aspects of the One Unity in which they are synthesized, so, in the manifested Universe, there is "that" which links spirit to matter, subject to object.

This something, at present unknown to Western speculation, is called by the occultists Fohat. It is the "bridge" by which the "Ideas" existing in the "Divine Thought" are impressed on Cosmic substance as the "laws of Nature."

Fohat is thus the dynamic energy of Cosmic Ideation; or, regarded from the other side, it is the intelligent medium, the guiding power of all manifestation, the "Thought Divine" transmitted and made manifest through the Dhyan Chohans,* the Architects of the visible World.

Thus from Spirit, or Cosmic Ideation, comes our consciousness; from Cosmic Substance the several vehicles in which that consciousness is individualised and attains to self -- or reflective -- consciousness; while Fohat, in its various manifestations, is the mysterious link between Mind and Matter, the animating principle electrifying every atom into life.

The following summary will afford a clearer idea to the reader.

(1.) The **ABSOLUTE**; the *Parabrahm* of the Vedantins or the one Reality, **SAT**, which is, as Hegel says, both Absolute Being and Non-Being.

(2.) The first manifestation, the impersonal, and, in philosophy, *unmanifested* Logos, the precursor of the "manifested." This is the "First Cause," the "Unconscious" of European Pantheists.

(3.) Spirit-matter, **LIFE**; the "Spirit of the Universe," the Purusha and Prakriti, or the *second* Logos.

(4.) Cosmic Ideation, **MAHAT** or Intelligence, the Universal World-Soul; the Cosmic Noumenon of Matter, the basis of the intelligent operations in and of Nature, also called **MAHA-BUDDHI**.

The **ONE REALITY**; its *dual* aspects in the conditioned Universe.

Further, the Secret Doctrine affirms: --

(b.) The Eternity of the Universe *in toto* as a boundless plane; periodically "the playground of numberless Universes incessantly manifesting and disappearing," called "the manifesting stars," and the "sparks of Eternity." "The Eternity of the Pilgrim"** is like a wink of the Eye of Self-Existence (Book of Dzyan.) "The appearance and disappearance of Worlds is like a regular tidal ebb of flux and reflux." (See Part II., "Days and Nights of Brahma.")

This second assertion of the Secret Doctrine is the absolute universality of that law of periodicity, of flux and reflux, ebb and flow, which physical science has observed and recorded in all departments of nature.

An alternation such as that of Day and Night, Life and Death, Sleeping and Waking, is a fact so common, so perfectly universal and without exception, that it is easy to comprehend that in it we see one of the absolutely fundamental laws of the universe.

Moreover, the Secret Doctrine teaches: --

(c) The fundamental identity of all Souls with the Universal Over-Soul, the latter being itself an aspect of the Unknown Root; and the obligatory pilgrimage for every Soul -- a spark of the former -- through the Cycle of Incarnation (or "Necessity") in accordance with Cyclic and Karmic law, during the whole term. In other words, no purely spiritual Buddhi (divine Soul) can have an independent (conscious) existence before the spark which issued from the pure Essence of the Universal Sixth principle, -- or the OVER-SOUL, -- has

(a) passed through every elemental form of the phenomenal world of that Manvantara, and

(b) acquired individuality, first by natural impulse, and then by self-induced and self-devised efforts (checked by its Karma), thus ascending through all the degrees of intelligence, from the lowest to the highest Manas, from mineral and plant, up to the holiest archangel (Dhyani-Buddha).

The pivotal doctrine of the Esoteric philosophy admits no privileges or special gifts in man, save those won by his own Ego through personal effort and merit throughout a long series of metempsychoses and reincarnations.

This is why the Hindus say that the Universe is Brahma and Brahmâ, for Brahma is in every atom of the universe, the six principles in Nature being all the outcome -- the variously differentiated aspects -- of the SEVENTH and ONE, the only reality in the Universe whether Cosmical or microcosmical; and also why the permutations (psychic, spiritual and physical), on the plane of manifestation and form, of the sixth (Brahmâ the vehicle of Brahma) are viewed by metaphysical."

If the reader would focus on these three observations repeatedly and with an open mind, the whole premise of the Secret Doctrine would open up.

Andras Nagy   February 2008

Murine Press

Please, visit our web site for further information and other great titles.

www.andras-nagy.com

Made in the USA